The Official
Celtic
Football Club
Annual 2007

Written by Dave O'Carroll

A Grange Publication

© 2006. Published by Grange Communications Ltd., Edinburgh, under licence from Celtic Football Club. Printed in the EU.

ISBN 0 9550057 0 1

£6.99

Contents

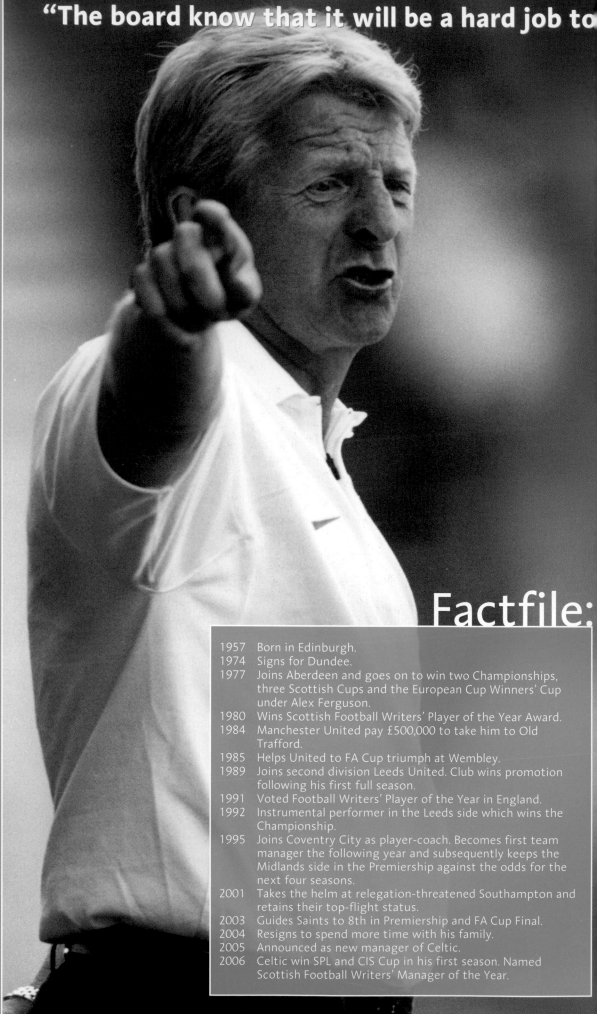

GORDON STRACHAN

Factfile:

1957	Born in Edinburgh.
1974	Signs for Dundee.
1977	Joins Aberdeen and goes on to win two Championships, three Scottish Cups and the European Cup Winners' Cup under Alex Ferguson.
1980	Wins Scottish Football Writers' Player of the Year Award.
1984	Manchester United pay £500,000 to take him to Old Trafford.
1985	Helps United to FA Cup triumph at Wembley.
1989	Joins second division Leeds United. Club wins promotion following his first full season.
1991	Voted Football Writers' Player of the Year in England.
1992	Instrumental performer in the Leeds side which wins the Championship.
1995	Joins Coventry City as player-coach. Becomes first team manager the following year and subsequently keeps the Midlands side in the Premiership against the odds for the next four seasons.
2001	Takes the helm at relegation-threatened Southampton and retains their top-flight status.
2003	Guides Saints to 8th in Premiership and FA Cup Final.
2004	Resigns to spend more time with his family.
2005	Announced as new manager of Celtic.
2006	Celtic win SPL and CIS Cup in his first season. Named Scottish Football Writers' Manager of the Year.

over from Martin and they believe I'm capable"
Gordon Strachan, May 2005

Hard job indeed. Martin O'Neill had won three SPL titles, three Scottish Cups, one CIS Cup and guided Celtic to the UEFA Cup Final during his five years in charge, ensuring legendary status amongst the Hoops' faithful. Gordon, however, knows a thing or two about winning. His glittering playing career at Aberdeen, Manchester United and Leeds United yielded silverware both north and south of the border as well as in Europe and, sure enough, within 12 months he had guided the Bhoys to the Championship, taking in a CIS Cup victory along the way. Not bad for your first season in charge.

The former English and Scottish Player of the Year (the only man to have won both awards) had a reputation as a fiery competitor on the field and it was not long before he needed to draw on those qualities in the wake of the club's exit from Europe at an early stage. Gordon was no stranger to adversity however following spells in charge of Coventry and Southampton. In fact, Southampton were second from bottom in the Premiership when he took the reigns. By the time he left, the club was still in the Premiership, had contested the FA Cup Final and been in the UEFA Cup.

The early setback was quickly forgotten as Celtic began their march towards the league title. Playing exciting football combined with strength and consistency, pacesetters Hearts were quickly overhauled and by the time the final whistle sounded on the last day of the campaign the Bhoys were 17 points clear.

A shrewd operator in the transfer market, his capture of Polish duo Maciej Zurawski and Artur Boruc may not have excited many headline writers initially but both kept them busy throughout their first season as Zurawski weighed in with 20 goals and Boruc quickly established himself as the Hoops' No.1. Surely the biggest coup was the signing of Irish superstar Roy Keane from under the noses of some of Europe's biggest clubs.

It has not all been about importing stars however. Gordon, who was capped more than 50 times for his country, has built a Celtic team with a strong Scottish presence. Stephen McManus is a regular in the first team as, of course is Shaun Maloney. Mark Wilson was signed from Dundee United in January 2006 whilst the capture of Gary Caldwell and Kenny Miller ensured this team of internationals would play with more of a Scottish heart.

Always good for a quote, Gordon Strachan has been a breath of fresh air in Scottish football and his impact has been acknowledged by the Scottish Football Writers Association when they named him as Manager of the Year at the end of his debut season. More importantly, they sing his name in the stands of Celtic Park.

July

30/07/05
Motherwell 4 Celtic 4
For the first game of the season, Celtic returned to Fir Park, the scene of that dramatic match on the last day of the 2004-05 campaign. This time the two sides served up a classic sharing eight goals in the process. Celtic had led 3-1 at the break - thanks to a John Hartson hat-trick - only to find themselves behind going into stoppage time. However a Hartson flick from a David Marshall long ball fell to Craig Beattie whose goal ensured a share of the points at the end of an incredible afternoon.

August

06/08/05
Celtic 2 Dundee United 0
Dundee United were visitors for the first home game of the SPL campaign, on the day when the Celtic faithful saw new signing Shunsuke Nakamura play for the first time. The Japanese international turned in a superb display to leave those in the stands buzzing with anticipation of the season ahead. Goals from Hartson and Beattie sealed a 2-0 win.

13/08/05
Celtic 3 Falkirk 1
Alan Thompson netted his first 2005/06 goals with a late brace in the defeat of Falkirk the following week. John Hartson had equalised for Celtic early in the second half before the Geordie stepped forward with two fine efforts. His first - a spectacular volley from outside the penalty area - was followed by a trademark free-kick curled around the defensive wall in the dying minutes of the game.

20/08/05
Rangers 3 Celtic 1
Two former team-mates faced each other in opposing dugouts for the first Old Firm game of the season. Gordon Strachan and Alex McLeish had enjoyed great success playing together as part of Alex Ferguson's all-conquering Aberdeen side in the 1980s and this was the first time they had pitted their wits against each other as managers. An evenly-matched contest was turned on its head when Alan Thompson was sent off midway through the first-half with the game scoreless. As it was, a late Shaun Maloney penalty was all the visiting support had to cheer as Rangers ran out 3-1 winners.

28/08/05
Dunfermline 0 Celtic 4
After the disappointment of the previous week, a comprehensive victory at East End Park meant the title challenge was back on track. Summer signing Maciej Zurawski helped himself to his first Celtic goal after only five minutes before claiming his second (and Celtic's fourth) in the second half. The other member of Celtic's new Polish double act, Artur Boruc, grabbed a few headlines of his own with a fine penalty save when there were only two goals between the teams. John Hartson (with his sixth league goal of the season) and Shunsuke Nakamura were also on target. The win moved Celtic to within five points of runaway leaders Hearts.

September

10/09/05
Celtic 2 Aberdeen 0
Aberdeen were the visitors to Glasgow when the SPL resumed following a break for international matches. Gordon Strachan's side swept aside the challenge of his former team with goals before and after the break from Maciej Zurawski and Stilian Petrov respectively. The match was preceded with one minute's applause to mark the 20th anniversary of the death of the legendary Jock Stein, a man the Celtic manager had played under whilst representing Scotland.

18/09/05
Hibernian 0 Celtic 1
Celtic moved into second place in the league following a hard-fought victory over Tony Mowbray's exciting young Hibs side at Easter Road. Stilian Petrov

Celtic

scored his second goal in as many games when he was put through by Nakamura and coolly slotted home with less than ten minutes gone. The second half was a much more even affair and Celtic had goalkeeper Artur Boruc to thank for keeping the home side at bay with some fine saves.

24/09/05
Celtic 2 Inverness Caledonian Thistle 1
Gordon Strachan handed striker Craig Beattie a rare start in this clash and his decision was justified as the young Scot scored twice to keep up the pressure on leaders Hearts. The Hoops had dominated the opening forty-five minutes without getting on the scoresheet and were made to pay when Wyness handed Caley a shock lead early in the second half. The advantage did not last long however and Beattie brought the Bhoys level just over five minutes later. Celtic had two penalty appeals turned down before Beattie settled matters with a well-taken goal.

October

01/10/05
Livingston 0 Celtic 5
Ex-Celt Paul Lambert's Livingston side were put to the sword as Celtic notched up their fifth straight league victory with five goals from five different players. Top scorer John Hartson was rested but it made little difference to the Hoops' firepower as Stephen MacManus and Shaun Maloney netted before the break to effectively put the result beyond doubt. Goals from Zurawski and Beattie, with Chris Sutton's first of the season sandwiched in between, completed the rout.

15/10/05
Celtic 1 Heart of Midlothian 1
Top-of-the-table Hearts began this eagerly-awaited clash match boasting an unbeaten record in the Premier League. As it was, both sides had to settle for a share of the points following a close encounter. Craig Beattie opened the scoring early in the first half controlling a Neil Lennon header across goal before firing into the roof of the net but the Edinburgh side responded quickly through Skacel. Celtic pressed hard but could not find a second goal. The result consolidated the Hoops' position in second place.

Celtic

November

23/10/05
Kilmarnock 0 Celtic 1

A Stilian Petrov strike midway through the first half was enough to see off Jim Jefferies' men at Rugby Park. The goal came following good work down the right from Paul Telfer who fed Chris Sutton. The big striker in turn squeezed a pass through to Petrov and the Bulgarian made no mistake from six yards. Celtic started this clash knowing that each of their rivals had won the day before so the three points were naturally important for Gordon Strachan's men.

26/10/05
Celtic 5 Motherwell 0

Celtic hit five for the second time in four matches and once again it was Stilian Petrov grabbing the headlines with his first hat-trick for the club. Any worries about the visit of Terry Butcher's men, who had proved to be a thorn in Celtic's side in their last two meetings, were quickly banished as Celts were three up midway through the first half thanks to two strikes from Petrov and another from Shaun Maloney. Indeed some of the link-up play between Celtic's two young Scots, Maloney and Beattie up front, had those in the stands purring with joy. A fine goal from Nakamura made it four before Stan ensured he would be taking the match ball home when he nudged in his third with just under 10 minutes remaining.

30/10/05
Dundee United 2 Celtic 4

Celts snatched the leadership of the SPL from Hearts following a great win at Tannadice. Gordon Strachan elected to go with Chris Sutton and John Hartson in attack and the old partnership came up trumps yet again. Following an early Sutton own-goal, Hartson quickly equalised before the Englishman made amends with an opportunistic strike. United equalised almost immediately but incredibly Celtic then re-took the lead less than two minutes later thanks to the second own goal of the game. Substitute Stephen Pearson scored his first of the season to wrap things up near the end.

06/11/05
Falkirk 0 Celtic 3

At the Falkirk Stadium, John Hartson scored his 100th goal for the club to keep the Bhoys in pole position in the title race. Celtic were never in any danger of slipping up as two goals in as many minutes from Aiden McGeady and Shaun Maloney had put the team two up by the break. The day belonged to the big Welshman however who put the seal on it with a well-executed volley. Afterwards the striker thanked his team-mates for helping him to reach the landmark total and spoke of his pride at joining that rather exclusive club.

19/11/05
Celtic 3 Rangers 0

The Old Firm met in the league at Celtic Park just 10 days after their CIS League Cup meeting and once again it was Celtic who emerged victorious. Alex McLeish had made numerous changes to the Rangers team whilst Gordon Strachan went with the same 11. John Hartson struck first after Shaun Maloney unselfishly played the striker in when he himself could have scored. Bobo Balde, from a Nakamura cross, made it 2-0 early in the second half before Aiden McGeady capped a superb display with an emphatic finish. The win meant the gap between the two great rivals had increased to 15 points.

26/11/05
Celtic 0 Dunfermline Athletic 1

Celtic suffered their first home league defeat of the season against a spirited Dunfermline side. The Fifers took the lead through Ross just after the quarter-hour mark and despite sustained possession Celtic struggled to create many clear opportunities. The only bright point for the home support on a bitterly cold afternoon was the return of Polish striker Maciej Zurawski (as a second half substitute) following a lengthy lay-off with a hamstring injury.

December

04/12/05

Aberdeen 1 Celtic 3

All four goals in this encounter were scored in a fifteen minute period during the second half. A reshuffled side fell behind to a Winters' strike just after the break but the goal only served to fire the Hoops into action and three goals in nine minutes, from McGeady, Petrov and Paul Telfer (his first for the club) guaranteed all three points. The result moved Celtic back to the top of the table.

10/12/05

Celtic 3 Hibernian 2

A crowd of almost 60,000 were served a real treat as Celtic edged out Hibs in a wonderful game which ebbed and flowed from start to finish. All was going to plan when Hartson headed in a Nakamura free-kick just before the break but two Hibs' goals at the beginning of the second forty-five stunned the home crowd. Celtic sparked into life and Maloney soon levelled with a marvellous free-kick. With the volume level turned up several notches, Celts searched for a winner and it duly arrived when Hartson converted a rebound after Maloney's shot came back off the post. Although Boruc had to race from his line to deny O'Connor in stoppage time, Celtic would not be denied.

18/12/05

Inverness Caledonian Thistle 1 Celtic 1

The travelling support, who spent most of their time before kick-off singing the name of new signing Roy Keane, were silenced when Caley took the lead after less than a minute. Hartson and Maloney both had chances to equalise before the big Welshman found the net just after the 20 minute mark following good work down the left from Ross Wallace. Both goalkeepers were forced to make crucial saves in the second period but a deciding goal never looked forthcoming.

26/12/05

Celtic 2 Livingston 1

The familiar name of Dalglish appeared on the scoresheet at Celtic Park but on this occasion it was Kenny's son Paul who equalised for visitors Livingston after a Maloney penalty had put the Hoops in front. On a frustrating afternoon it took a moment of magic from Nakamura (with only a couple of minutes remaining) to unlock the opposing defence and ensure the Bhoys would end the year in exactly the same position they began 2005 - at the top of the SPL table.

January

01/01/06
Hearts 2 Celtic 3
A dramatic afternoon at Tynecastle ended with the gap between Scotland's top two increased to seven points. Centre-half Stephen McManus was the somewhat unlikely hero with two goals in the last five minutes to snatch victory from the jaws of defeat for a Celtic team two goals behind with less than 10 minutes on the clock. Stephen Pearson, on for the injured Petrov, had pulled one back early in the second half. Step forward McManus who twice converted Nakamura free-kicks to hand the Hoops the win, and take a decisive step in the race for the title.

14/01/06
Celtic 4 Kilmarnock 2
Roy Keane made his home debut with an assured performance in defence as Celts stretched their unbeaten run in the league to six matches. Strikes from Nakamura and Maloney (a penalty) within the first quarter of an hour appeared to set up a comfortable afternoon but Naismith pulled one back before Invincible made it 2-2 early in the second half. McManus then ensured that parity would not be restored for long with his third in two games before Zurawski put the result beyond doubt with a tidy close-range finish.

22/01/06
Motherwell 1 Celtic 3
With three central defenders unavailable Celtic began with the untried partnership of Stanislav Varga and Adam Virgo at the back. Varga was making his first start since the 4-4 draw at Fir Park on opening day, but there would be no repeat of that afternoon's theatre as goals from Zurawski, McGeady and Hartson completed the win. The gap at the top of the SPL was now 10 points.

28/01/06
Celtic 3 Dundee United 3
Gordon Strachan's men scored three times for the fourth consecutive league game but only managed a draw as United, inspired by ex-Celt David Fernandez, scored twice in the last 10 minutes to grab a point. Thanks to another superb Nakamura free-kick Hartson headed Celtic in front only for Fernandez to equalise before the break. Goals from Zurawski and Petrov established a two-goal advantage that appeared to kill the game before Fernandez (again) and Miller struck late for the Tangerines.

February

08/02/06

Celtic 2 Falkirk 1

The gap between the Hoops and their closest challengers was increased on the night that Roy Keane scored his first for the club. Just over half an hour had elapsed when the Irishman pounced on a half-cleared free-kick to smash the ball home from outside the box. McManus made it two just over ten minutes later after collecting a Maloney cross and firing into the roof of the net. A Milne strike for the visitors ensured a nervy last 10 minutes for the home support.

12/02/06

Rangers 0 Celtic 1

At the home of their great rivals Celtic produced a commanding performance which subsequently opened up a 21-point gap between them. With Keane and skipper Neil Lennon in imperious form, Celts had control of the game from an early stage and once in front dominated the play. Early on, Zurawski nipped in for the only goal - his 11th of the season, when he reacted quickest to a blocked Petrov effort.

19/02/06

Dunfermline 1 Celtic 8

The travelling supporters who made the journey to Fife were treated to an incredible display that featured four goals from Maciej Zurawski and the rare sight of a Neil Lennon strike hitting the back of the net. Celtic were in front after less than five minutes through Stan Petrov before Tod levelled for the Pars. Hartson restored the advantage before his Polish strike partner put the game beyond doubt with two goals prior to half-time. Early in the second half the front two linked well and the Welshman set up 'Magic' for his hat-trick. Maloney scored the pick of the bunch with a fabulous volley before Lennon claimed his first goal in four years with a curling shot from outside the area. Amazingly there was still time for the Polish striker to net his fourth and complete a wonderful afternoon's work in the Kingdom.

March

04/03/06

Celtic 3 Aberdeen 0

Three second period goals were enough to see off Aberdeen and condemn Jimmy Calderwood's side to their first league defeat of the year. Although Celtic had the better of the match throughout, the deadlock was not broken until mid-way through the second half when a Zurawski cut-back was clinically dispatched into the net by Petrov. Maloney doubled the advantage from close range ten minutes later. As Aberdeen faded a third was added late on when a spell of possession football on the edge of the box set up Zurawski for his sixth goal in just three games.

12/03/06

Hibernian 1 Celtic 2

Those leaving Easter Road could be forgiven for letting their thoughts wander towards a Championship party as this victory meant the gap between Celtic and the other side from the capital was 15 points with nine matches to go. Even with such a commanding lead however, Celts still had to display fine battling qualities to come from behind and take all three points. Riordan gave the home side the lead before a strong burst from Maloney was illegally stopped when the striker was upended in the area. The young Scot himself stroked the penalty home. Celtic found it tough to break down Hibs with centre-half Gary Caldwell's display demonstrating just why Gordon Strachan had already moved to bring him to Parkhead for Season 2006/07. McManus popped up with the decisive strike, prodding the ball home from a corner.

22/03/06

Celtic 2 Inverness Caledonian Thistle 1

This was the first home fixture since the death of Jimmy Johnstone and the event was marked by his Lisbon Lions team-mates appearing alongside his wife Agnes before kick-off to celebrate the life of the wing wizard. Stephen McManus continued his fine goalscoring form with a powerful header just after the 30-minute mark. This was his eighth goal of the season and a fine return for a centre-back. A textbook Maloney free-kick put the result beyond doubt with just over 10 minutes

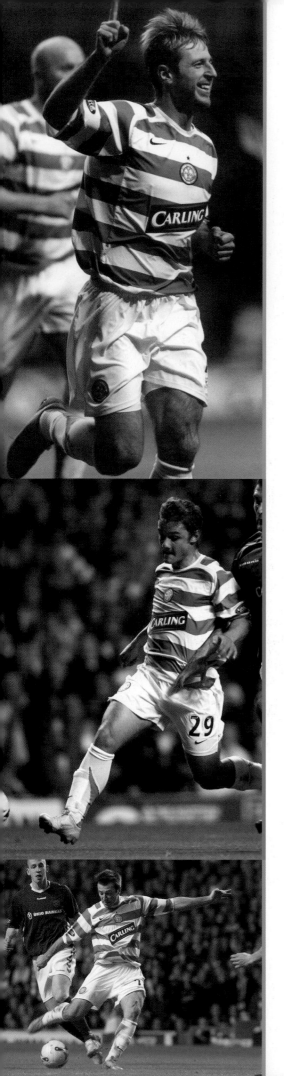

remaining. Hart scored a late consolation for the visitors but Celtic now had the winning line clearly in their sights.

26/03/06
Livingston 0 Celtic 2

The SPL's bottom club had given the top sides some scares already during the season and the Bhoys had to fight hard for this victory. Both teams came close early on with Artur Boruc needing to be sharp to keep the home side out. Once again it was his Polish international team-mate Zurawski who grabbed the vital breakthrough. Less than a minute after the restart he stabbed the ball home following good work by Ross Wallace. A foul on Dion Dublin inside the box presented Maloney with the chance to double the lead and he made no mistake from the spot. The three points meant victory over second-place Hearts in their next match would guarantee that the title would be returning to Celtic Park.

April

05/04/06
Celtic 1 Hearts 0

A John Hartson goal was enough to clinch the SPL Championship as Hearts' strong challenge was finally seen off. Just a day after celebrating his 31st birthday, the big Welshman set the scene for another party with a long-range effort after less than five minutes. The Tynecastle side came back strongly in an attempt to keep their slim title aspirations alive but could not break down Celts' resolute defence.. Manager Gordon Strachan had now emulated his predecessor Martin O'Neill by winning the league at his first attempt.

09/04/06
Kilmarnock 1 Celtic 4

The ultimate goal had been achieved but the Bhoys showed they were not about to take their foot off the pedal as they hit four past an improving Kilmarnock side. A stunning free-kick from Nakamura opened the scoring after less than 10 minutes. The Japanese has proved himself to be a master of dead-ball situations and in both he and Maloney, the Hoops have two players who are extremely dangerous from outside the area. Hartson made it two before Naka netted his second from six yards when he finished off a fabulous team move. Dion Dublin made it four with a well-executed finish before Killie's late consolation through Nish.

16/04/06
Celtic 1 Hibernian 1
Jubilation abounded at Celtic Park as the team were presented with the Championship trophy in front of a crowd of over 60,000. Comedian and Celtic fan Billy Connolly was given the honour of presenting captain Neil Lennon and manager Gordon Strachan with the silverware to the acclaim of the green-and-white faithful. On the pitch, Hibs became the first side since Dundee United back in January to take a point off the Hoops as Zurawski, who had been his usual constant threat throughout, cancelled out Fletcher's opener.

23/04/06
Celtic 0 Rangers 0
The final Old Firm encounter was a rather lifeless affair lacking all the spark that this fixture usually generates. Artur Boruc made some smart stops as the visitors tried to give their boss a win in his last game against Celtic but the Polish international never really looked like losing a goal. Maloney created problems up front forcing Wattereus into a good save with a long range effort.

30/04/06
Hearts 3 Celtic 0
Celtic were always going to find it tough against a Hearts side still fighting for second place and so it proved as two early goals left the Hoops with just too much to do. Incidentally, this defeat was Celtic's first in a league game since the reversal at home to Dunfermline in November, a run spanning 20 matches.

May

03/05/06
Celtic 2 Kilmarnock 0
Six changes were made to the starting line up as the Champions won their last home game of the season. Celts were always in control with the duo of Keane and McGeady in sparkling form. However, it was one of the manager's first signings for the club, Zurawski, who made the breakthrough in the second half with his 20th goal since his move from Wisla Cracow in July 2005. Stan Varga added a second less than 10 minutes later with a back post header from a Wallace cross for the Hoops'14th home win.

07/05/06
Aberdeen 2 Celtic 2
The final match of the season saw Celtic travel north to the Granite City with the sides playing out an entertaining draw and sharing four goals. Hartson joined strike partner Zurawski on the 20 goal mark when, early in the match, he reacted quickly to nod home a stinging McGeady shot which rebounded off the bar. Shaun Maloney capped a wonderful season with a fine individual effort after the break, when the newly-crowned Player of the Year took on the entire Dons' defence before unleashing a rasping drive from outside the area. Two Stewart goals meant the match finished all-square and signalled the end of an immensely satisfying campaign for the Champions.

16

01 What was Celtic's final points tally for the campaign?

02 The final goal of the league season was registered at Pittodrie, who scored it?

03 Which ex-Celt scored twice for his new club at Celtic Park?

04 Which team were hit for eight in February 2006?

05 Which Hoops star scored four goals in that game?

06 The only SPL side to score four times in a single game against Celtic were ...?

07 Against which club did Roy Keane make his SPL debut?

08 Celtic's first goal of 2006 was scored by whom?

09 How many league goals did John Hartson score last season?

10 Which defender scored twice against Hearts at Tynecastle?

11 Who played both for and against Celtic in season 2005/06?

12 Only one of the top six teams were beaten four times by Celtic, which?

At the end of the 2005/06 campaign Shaun Maloney created history when he became the first player to win the PFA Player of the Year and Young Player of the Year awards in the same season. The achievement was all the more remarkable considering the 23-year-old spent the best part of a year out of the game having suffered a cruciate ligament injury in February 2004. The glittering array of prizes bestowed upon him was just reward for his determination and will to succeed.

He was just 15-years-old when he signed 'S' forms for Celtic having already been approached by Hearts and both Dundee clubs. Upon leaving school aged 16, he joined the Hoops full-time and a mere two years later he was appearing in the senior side.

The striker made his debut for Celtic as a substitute in a 3-0 victory over Rangers in April 2001. Under Martin O'Neill the youngster made frequent appearances without ever really cementing a place in the starting 11. However, he seemed destined to make that final step to firmly establish himself in the manager's plans when he suffered the knee injury during an under-21 match against Partick Thistle.

Despite that setback, the club had confidence in their young starlet and demonstrated this by offering a new three-year contract in May 2004. After slowly working his way back to full fitness Maloney repaid their faith with a number of breathtaking performances and stunning goals during Gordon Strachan's first season in charge.

A dynamic, exciting player, Maloney echoes heroes of the past with his tricky runs and excellent close control. His blistering 40-yard effort against Rangers in the CIS Cup match in 2005/06 will be talked about for years. His prowess in dead-ball situation is such that the Parkhead crowds could be forgiven for losing count of the number of times they have seen a free-kick dispatched straight into the net from his boot, such as his strike in the 2006 CIS League Cup Final.

In all, Celts' no. 29 scored 16 goals during the campaign - finishing as the club's third-top-scorer - as well as providing numerous assists for his team mates. He has also broken into the international set-up, having been a regular at under-21 level for many years, and will surely become a fixture of the Scotland team in the years to come.

In an area dominated by foreign superstars, it bodes well for Scottish football that one of the hottest properties in the game is a young Scot busy rewriting history at the club he joined as a teenager. Celtic supporters all over the world are surely looking forward to many more seasons watching him on the edge of their seats.

19

Spot the Difference

Study the two pictures below and try to spot the 12 differences between them (we've given you a start with the first difference). Answers on page 61.

CHAMPIONSHIP TREBLE

Celtic's Under-19 Youth team emulated the senior side by winning their league Championship last season. The reserve team's subsequent title success meant the club achieved a stunning treble in Season 2005/06 and one which, in the words of chief executive Peter Lawwell, "gives us tremendous hope for the future".

Under-19 coach Willie McStay had every reason to be proud of his side as they clinched their fourth consecutive Youth Team Championship with three games to spare. As if that was not enough, his charges made it a league and cup double when they defeated Hearts 3-1 after extra-time in the Youth Cup Final at Celtic Park. Amazingly this was the third year in a row that the league and Cup double had been captured at Under-19 level, a fact which keenly illustrates the fantastic job being done by Willie and his assistant Joe McBride. McStay typically deflected all attention away from himself saying the "most pleasing aspect is when the manager (Gordon Strachan) is commenting on the style of play and praising the boys".

The youth team boss has been unearthing great talents at Celtic for over 12 years and has seen many young stars go on to play for the first team and be capped at international level. He has bridged the gap to the first team to such an extent that it would not be a surprise to see some of the class of 2005/06 emulating former youth team players such as Shaun Maloney, Aiden McGeady and Stephen McManus by becoming regulars for the Hoops.

The final piece of Celtic's title treble was sealed by the reserve team who won their Championship for the fifth year in succession. The team managed by Kenny McDowell and his assistant, Celts legend Danny McGrain, enjoyed an especially satisfying campaign as they were victorious with a particularly young group of players this time around.

The reserve team has played a vital role in facilitating the transition for talented youngsters from Under-19 level to the senior side. The wonderful achievement of Celtic teams at all three levels in proving themselves to be the best in Scotland not only ensured much celebration last season but gave a firm indication that many more will surely follow in the future.

Celtic

JIMMY JOHNSTONE

Most great clubs across the world have one player whose name is spoken only in adoration. One of whom older generations tell stories and younger fans wish they had seen in the flesh. One who ends any 'greatest player' arguments as soon as they enter the conversation. Players like Johan Cruyff of Ajax, Alfredo Di Stefano of Real Madrid, George Best of Manchester United… and Jimmy Johnstone of Celtic.

Even today the grainy footage of the man called 'Jinky' produces gasps from the viewer. The wee man from Viewpark turned defenders inside out with his wizardry. Big bruising defenders from all over Europe set out to kick him out of the game but found themselves kicking only thin air. The 5ft 4inch midfielder with the red hair became a legend.

Jimmy Johnstone signed for Celtic in 1963 but it was not until the arrival of the great Jock Stein two years later that he began to have a prolonged run in the side. Stein wanted to create a team where everyone was comfortable with the ball at their feet and Johnstone was the jewel in the crown. His relationship with the manager was pivotal to the Hoops success. Big Jock knew how to handle him.

One famous story concerned a European tie against Red Star Belgrade. A notoriously bad flyer, Jimmy had asked Stein not to take him on the long plane journey to Yugoslavia for the second leg. Big Jock told him he could stay at home if Celtic had a comfortable enough lead after the first match. Jinky subsequently scored two and set up three of Celtic's five goals that night. It is claimed that in conversation with Stein after the match, the Red Star manager begged the Celts' boss to take Jinky to Belgrade so his countrymen could see him in action.

His style won over opposition players and fans alike. Former Liverpool and England captain Emlyn Hughes once said he "loved to hate" playing against him. Jimmy was even asked to play at the great Alfredo Di Stefano's tribute game in Madrid where his performance had the 125,000 crowd in the Bernabeu crying "Olé" in delight.

The high point of his career came on that famous evening in 1967 when he was part of the team that became the first British Club to win the European Cup. During his time at Celtic Park he also won nine Championships, four Scottish Cups and five League Cups. In over 500 appearances for the club he scored 129 goals.

In later years Jinky was regularly seen at Celtic Park much to the jubilation of his adoring fans who had voted him Celtic's greatest-ever player. His modest and friendly nature meant he was well liked by more modern greats such as Henrik Larsson with whom he became good friends.

Jimmy Johnstone died in March 2006 after a long battle with motor neurone disease. The outpouring of grief and the depth of tributes to the man from all over the world showed the affection in which he was held and ensured that his legend will live forever.

Name:	Celtic Park
Capacity:	60,832
Record attendance:	92,000 (v. Rangers 1938)
Average attendance 05/06:	58,149
Nickname:	Paradise
Opened:	1892

Fact: The North Stand alone can hold nearly 27,000 people, more than can be accommodated in 10 SPL stadiums and five in the English Premiership.

Season 2006/2007 fixtures

29/07/06 – Kilmarnock (H)
06/08/06 – Hearts (A)
12/08/06 – St Mirren (H)
20/08/06 – Inverness CT (A)
26/08/06 – Hibernian (H)
09/09/06 – Aberdeen (A)
16/09/06 – Dunfermline (H)
23/09/06 – Rangers (H)
01/10/06 – Falkirk (A)
14/10/06 – Dundee United (A)
21/10/06 – Motherwell (H)
28/10/06 – Kilmarnock (A)
04/11/06 – Hearts (H)
12/11/06 – St Mirren (A)
18/11/06 – Inverness CT (H)
26/11/06 – Hibernian (A)
02/12/06 – Aberdeen (H)

10/12/06 – Dunfermline (A)
16/12/06 – Rangers (A)
23/12/06 – Falkirk (H)
26/12/06 – Dundee United (H)
30/12/06 – Motherwell (A)
01/01/07 – Kilmarnock (H)
14/01/07 – Hearts (A)
20/01/07 – St Mirren (H)
28/01/07 – Inverness CT (A)
10/02/07 – Hibernian (H)
17/02/07 – Aberdeen (A)
03/03/07 – Dunfermline (H)
10/03/07 – Rangers (H)
17/03/07 – Falkirk (A)
31/03/07 – Dundee United (A)
07/04/07 – Motherwell (H)

SPL splits into top six and bottom six. Final fixtures to be announced after April 7th. Fixtures are subject to change.

01 How many times did Celtic qualify for the group stages under Martin O'Neill?

02 Who was Celtic's first qualifying match in the Champions League against and what was the score?

03 Name the striker (he went on to play for the Hoops), who helped Croatia Zagreb eliminate Celtic in a qualifier in 1998?

04 Which three players scored in the famous 4-3 victory over Juventus in October 2001?

05 Which Belgian side conceded three goals in the first 30 minutes of a group encounter in Glasgow in 2003?

06 Before Season 2006/07, who scored Celtic's last goal in the group stages?

07 In the same match which African superstar became the last player to score against the Hoops in a group match before this season?

08 Four different players scored in the 4-0 win over Artmedia Bratislava last season, name them.

09 Celtic qualified for the group stages for the first time with a famous 3-1 win over Ajax in Amsterdam, but which future Rangers player scored the Dutch team's goal that night?

10 Which Irish midfielder scored goals against Lyon and Anderlecht during the group stage in 2003?

Every goal scored by a man in a Celtic shirt is memorable for one reason or another but here are 5 special efforts from the 2006/06 campaign we thought you would like to be reminded of:

Shaun Maloney v. Dunfermline, East End Park, 19/02/06

In a season of special goals the Scottish PFA Player of the Year outdid himself with this effort on a day when it rained goals in Fife. Zurawski picked the ball up close to the right touchline and advanced forward before launching a cross-field ball. Maloney stood on the edge of the penalty area facing the Polish striker's pass as it arched towards him. Demonstrating incredible agility and technique, the Scot turned his body and volleyed the ball whilst in mid-air, sending it flying into the top corner of the Pars' net. The subsequent celebrations from both fans and team-mates illustrated just how special a goal they had all just witnessed.

Shunsuke Nakamura v. Livingston, Celtic Park, 26/12/05

The Japanese International demonstrated superb ability from free-kicks throughout the season but this Boxing Day Special was arguably his best goal from open play. With the scores level at one each, the resolute Livvy defence was proving to be difficult to break down and with time running out it began to look like the home side would have to settle for a point. Collecting the ball in the inside right channel, the midfielder turned neatly and ran at the retreating defenders. He beat one man before cutting inside swiftly to evade a second challenge. As a third defender charged towards him he unleashed a blistering left-foot strike from 18 yards to beat the 'keeper at the near post and win the game for the Hoops.

John Hartson v. Hearts, Celtic Park, 05/04/06

This sweetly-struck volley will go down in history as the goal which secured the SPL title. Celtic Park was packed for this midweek fixture and there was huge anticipation in the air as the teams occupying the top two positions locked horns. With less than five minutes played the Jambos' defence failed to deal with a Boruc goal kick, the ball bounced to Zurawski and he nodded it in the direction of the big Welshman who hammered it first time on the volley from over 25 yards past the despairing dive of Scotland international goalkeeper Craig Gordon, sending the home support into raptures.

Maciej Zurawski v.Kilmarnock, Celtic Park, 03/05/06

This end-of-season encounter was lit up by a fine team goal with contributions from Keane and Petrov amongst others before "Magic" supplied the finishing touch. Early in the second half the Killie defence seemed in little danger as Celtic held the ball inside their own half. Within seconds though they had been cut open in a move reminiscent of Carlos Alberto's famous goal for Brazil in 1970 as, following a series of passes though the middle of the park, the ball reached full-back Wilson who fired it across the goal where the No. 7 was waiting to despatch the ball into the roof of the goal.

Shaun Maloney v. Rangers, Celtic Park, 09/11/05
A stunning individual effort which astounded many inside Celtic Park as well as those watching on television. This cup match between the old foes was characteristically tight and cautious prior to this moment of magic. Picking the ball up in his own half the young Scot ran at the Rangers defence. As defenders backed off waiting to see what he would do he belted a 40-yard scorcher past Klos into the Rangers net. Goals against Rangers are especially appreciated by Hoops fans and it is certain they will be talking about this one for years to come.

Kenny Miller is just the third post-war player to have played for both Celtic and Rangers. Alfie Conn and Maurice Johnston were the other two.

Shaun Maloney was born in Malaysia. He was four when his family moved back to Scotland.

Celtic Park is the second biggest club stadium in Britain. Only Manchester United's Old Trafford can accommodate more fans.

Paul Telfer is the nephew of former Dundee United, Chelsea and Scotland ace Eamonn Bannon.

John Hartson is bilingual having attended a Welsh speaking school.

The last Scottish Celtic player to win the PFA Players' Player of the Year Award before Shaun Maloney was Jackie McNamara in 1998.

Celtic's most capped player is goalkeeper Pat Bonner, who played 80 times for the Republic of Ireland. Paul McStay is the most capped Scot with 76 appearances.

Two of Neil Lennon's three Celtic goals have been scored at the same ground - East End Park, Dunfermline.

Celtic currently hold the SPL record for longest unbeaten run at home (77 matches) and longest run of wins in a single season (25 matches).

31

Artur Boruc

The 6ft 4in stopper was initially signed by Gordon Strachan from Legia Warsaw in July 2005 on a season-long loan but such was his talent that it was not long before he had established himself as the manager's first choice goalkeeper and signed a contract to keep him at the club for another three years.

Hailing from Siedlce in Poland, the 26-year-old was an integral part of the championship winning side with a string of impressive displays which included shut-outs against each of the Hoops' main rivals. In total, he made 40 appearances for the team in his first season.

Artur's displays led to a call-up for the Poland squad for the 2006 World Cup at the expense of the more established Jerzy Dudek.

David Marshall

Despite falling behind Boruc in the pecking order, the young Glaswegian remains one of the most exciting prospects in the Scottish game. He became an instant hit when he produced a nerveless display at the Nou Camp against mighty Barcelona in March 2004 and followed this with another wonderful performance a few days later at Ibrox, ensuring his heroic status amongst the Hoops fans.

A product of the Celtic youth system, the 21-year-old has also been capped for Scotland. Proof, if any were needed, of the big future lying ahead with both club and country.

Dianbobo Balde

Season 2006/07 will be the big defender's sixth in Glasgow since his move from Toulouse. Indeed such has been the measure of the contribution of 'Bobo', that it is almost difficult to remember a time when the Celtic defence was not marshalled by his dominating presence.

The Guinea international has always attracted envious glances from top Premiership and European sides but he remains the immovable figure in Celtic's back four with over 200 appearances in the number 6 shirt. A constant goal threat from set pieces, his hulking physique has proved to be a headache for opposition attackers and defenders alike.

To date, he has won three league championships, two Scottish Cups and one CIS Cup during his time at Celtic.

Stephen McManus

The young man from Lanark has come through the ranks at Celtic Park to establish himself in the first 11. A strong defender, he has formed a good understanding with Balde in the Celtic defence. However, arguably his biggest contribution has been at the other end of the pitch where he has demonstrated an incredible knack of scoring vital goals in important matches.

Surely the best example of this was on New Year's Day 2006 when, with Celtic trailing 2-1 to nearest challengers Hearts, he twice converted Nakamura free-kicks in the last five minutes to win the game and put clear daylight between the top two.

He repeated the trick in the Capital by also scoring the winner against Hibernian and ended the season with eight goals to his name - a remarkable tally for a central defender.

Paul Telfer

Once in charge Gordon Strachan made Paul Telfer one of his first acquisitions. The attack-minded right back had played under him at both Coventry and Southampton, where his willingness to get forward and provide dangerous delivery from the wing won many admirers, so it was no surprise when the manager moved to bring him north to Glasgow.

With over 40 appearances and a Championship medal in his first season, it is fair to assume that the player is delighted that he did.

Mark Wilson

The young defender fulfilled a boyhood dream when he signed for Celtic in January 2006. His impressive displays for Dundee United had persuaded the Celtic hierarchy to make a move for the Glaswegian and the lifelong Celtic fan needed little persuasion. He went on to play 14 times during the rest of the season.

As a former captain of the Scotland under-21 side and one of many exciting young Scottish players plying their trade at Celtic, it is surely only a matter of time before he is established as a regular in the international set-up.

Neil Lennon

Signed from Leicester City by Martin O'Neill in December 2000, the man from Lurgan has been one of the club's most distinguished servants over the last few years racking up nearly 300 appearances in the process. At the beginning of the 2005/06 season he was handed the captain's armband by Gordon Strachan.

A strong, combative presence in the midfield, the skipper has been courted by many other top clubs but has remained in Glasgow, where he enjoys a unique bond with the Celtic support. This decision was justified as he lifted the SPL Championship trophy and the CIS Cup in his first season with the captaincy.

Shunsuke Nakamura

The Japanese international took little time in impressing as he was voted man of the match on his debut against Dundee United. A wonderful exponent of the dead-ball, the midfielder has set up numerous goals for his team mates with his delivery from free-kicks. Allied to this, his ability to spot a killer pass has left defences throughout the SPL bedraggled as they struggled to cope with him.

Capped over 50 times for Japan, it was his performances for the national side in the 2005 Confederations Cup that persuaded Gordon Strachan to prise him away from Italian side Reggina. He was selected as a member of his country's squad for the World Cup in Germany and scored his country's first goal in the finals.

Craig Beattie

The pacey striker struggled with injury during the last campaign but still managed seven goals including the last-gasp equaliser at Fir Park on opening day. The youngster caught the eye playing for Celtic's youth and under-21 sides and is fast approaching 100 appearances for the senior side. His quick progress through the ranks at Celtic Park has not gone unnoticed at international level and he has been called upon to represent Scotland since his breakthrough.

Stilian Petrov

The longest serving player in the current squad, 'Stan' was signed by John Barnes from CSKA Sofia in his native Bulgaria. During his time at Celtic Park he has matured into one of the most influential players in Scotland, with lavish praise being heaped upon him from both the media and the terraces.

A powerhouse of a player, surging runs and strong tackling are a feature of his game and his goal return is impressive for a midfielder - he has rarely failed to hit double figures in a season. With over 50 Caps for his country he is captain of the Bulgarian national side.

Aiden McGeady

uch is the talent of this prodigious youngster that
e was already being talked about as a future star
efore he had played a single match. Then again,
his was no surprise for a player who has seemed
head of his time ever since he was selected for a
lasgow under-11 team at the age of seven.

is quick feet and trickery have since shone on a
igger stage as he has turned in man of the match
isplays against the likes of AC Milan amongst
thers. Although hampered by injury in Season
005/06, he still managed four SPL goals, including
ne against Rangers. The Glasgow-born winger
pted to declare for the Republic of Ireland (he
ualifies through his grandparents) whilst at
choolboy level and has since picked up full caps.
here is no doubt he will be thrilling the crowds at
eltic for years to come.

Maciej Zurawski

The No.7 shirt is special for Celtic fans. It conjures up happy memories of Jimmy Johnstone and Henrik Larsson and, as such, whoever wears it is subject to particular scrutiny. Just as well that the latest incumbent happens to be a goal-machine who proved in just one season that he has no trouble finding the net. 'Magic' scored 20 goals in his debut year, a great achievement for anyone, let alone a player from Eastern Europe unaccustomed to the Scottish game.

Signed from Wisla Krakow in summer 2005, it did not take long for the Polish international to begin improving Celtic's 'goals for' column, initially scoring in his fifth game. He even managed to score four goals in a single match as well as notching a winner at Ibrox – a sure way to endear yourself to the Hoops' support. Not surprisingly he was selected for the Polish squad for the World Cup.

Kenny Miller

The most experienced of Gordon Strachan's new Scottish trio, the striker signed a deal in January to move to Glasgow from Wolves for the 2006/07 season. Celtic beat a number of clubs to the signature of the player who has enjoyed something of a revival in his career since he left Scotland to move south. Edinburgh-born Miller hit 24 goals as Wolves gained promotion to the Premiership in 2002/03 and although they only lasted one season in the top flight he caught the eye with goals against Liverpool and Manchester United.

This form helped him regain his international place and his performances for the national team - a goal against Italy quickly followed by two in Norway - brought many admirers and once it became clear he would be leaving the Midlands for a new challenge there was no shortage of interested parties.

However it was Celtic who persuaded the former Hibs and Rangers man to return home. The Hoops manager believes the player still has his "best years ahead of him".

See if you can find the 15 words contained within the grid from the clues below. Words can appear horizontally, vertically or diagonally.

B	W	M	T	L	A	R	S	S	O	N	F
C	G	I	A	P	D	J	B	A	I	Q	E
L	A	L	X	S	T	E	I	N	B	H	A
T	M	L	P	A	R	A	D	I	S	E	H
F	B	E	M	V	N	H	U	C	Q	R	M
S	H	R	A	K	I	J	B	D	T	J	C
B	O	B	I	Z	C	A	L	I	O	N	S
O	Y	P	K	O	U	I	I	O	K	W	T
R	S	T	A	N	L	R	N	T	P	Z	A
U	K	B	H	E	N	J	A	X	J	J	Y
C	S	Q	A	I	Q	W	H	W	R	I	E
L	T	R	J	L	R	V	V	L	S	N	W
F	I	P	G	L	G	T	K	I	Z	K	O
C	R	I	R	Y	K	W	E	H	M	Y	I
H	U	D	D	L	E	F	X	E	Y	U	G
S	X	B	V	F	D	K	U	V	N	T	S

Clues:

1. Celtic Park by another name
2. Stilian's nickname
3. Irish capital, Celtic striker
4. Not ghirls
5. Legendary manager
6. Lisbon animals
7. Strachan's predecessor
8. He's "magic"
9. Number of league cup triumphs
10. Ritual before kick-off
11. Jimmy Johnstone's nickname
12. Legendary Swedish no.7
13. Pole in the goal
14. Celtic's most-capped Scot
15. Scotland international striker signed from Wolves

The names below have been jumbled up. Can you figure out who we are talking about?

01 Captain in Lisbon 1967 – Limb cell lyin

02 Player of the year in Season 2005/06 – Yu has non lame

03 The boss – Don ran ghost car

04 Midfielder, has a "nak" with free-kicks – U make sarah unsunk

05 Has played for the manager at three different clubs – Falter up el

06 Glasgow-born goalkeeper – Valid hard slam

07 Wing wizard – GI Cayman deed

08 Defender signed from Hibernian – Drawl clay gel

09 6ft 4 Czech midfielder – Sir Jaki Jiro

10 Hoops' no.33 – Call was sore

CIS CUP

CIS Cup

Celtic claimed the CIS League Cup for the 13th time last season disposing of Falkirk, Rangers and Motherwell along the way before facing Dunfermline on an emotional March day at Hampden. This was the Bhoys' first triumph in the competition since season 2000/01.

CIS Cup 3rd Round – Celtic 2 Falkirk 1
(after extra time)

Celts had to come from behind to overcome the battling Bairns who had been thrashed 8-1 at the same stage in the competition the year before. There was to be no repeat of that one-sided encounter however as John Hughes' men began the game in dogged mood. In fact, it was the visitors who took the lead early in the second half but it only took Celtic nine minutes to draw level when Maciej Zurawski fired home. With no more scoring in the ninety minutes the tie was decided early in extra time when John Hartson rose to power a trademark header into the visitors' net and send Celtic into the next round.

CIS Cup 4th Round – Celtic 2 Rangers 0

There was no doubting that the tie of the 4th round was the Old Firm head-to-head at Celtic Park. The home side gave manager Gordon Strachan his first victory over their Glasgow rivals with a blistering performance that was lit up by a wonder goal from Shaun Maloney. Midway through the first half, the youngster gathered in his own half and headed for the Rangers goal. Some thirty yards out he let fly and the ball screamed past Klos as the Celtic masses celebrated one of the best-ever derby goals between the two great rivals.

With Rangers down to ten men for much of the second period after the dismissal of Kyrgiakos, Celtic struck again with less than ten minutes remaining when the powerful presence of Bobo Balde forced Klos to put through his own net. The celebrations were now in full swing as the home support anticipated a trip to Hampden for the semi-final.

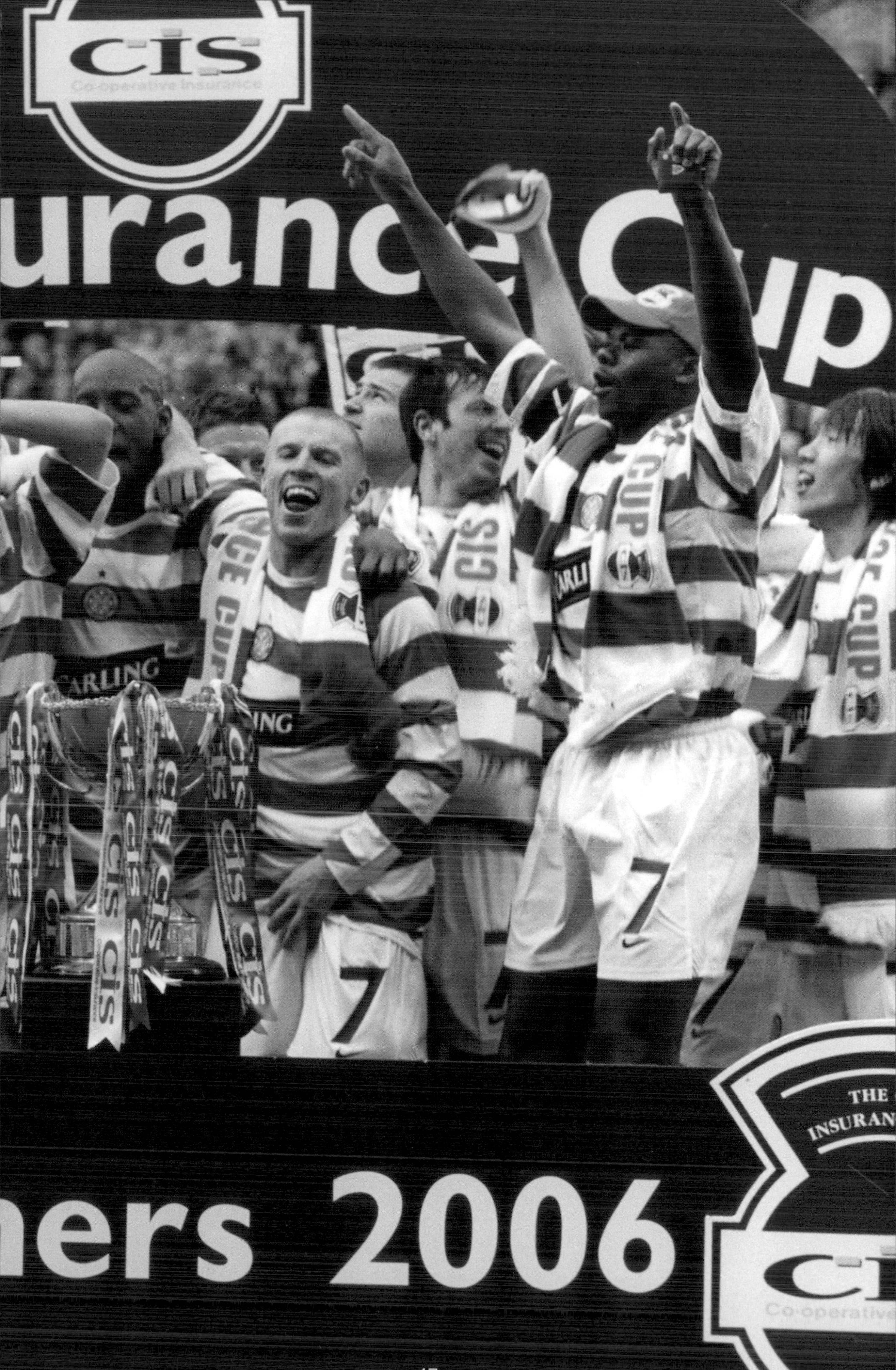
CIS
Co-operative Insurance
urance Cup
ners 2006

CIS Cup Semi-final – Motherwell 1 Celtic 2

Once again, Celtic came from behind after Foran had headed Terry Butcher's side into an early lead at the national stadium before Zurawski levelled the match with a low shot 16 minutes later. With clear-cut chances proving difficult to come by for both sides the game seemed destined for extra-time, however there was still drama to unfold. First Artur Boruc produced a marvellous save from Kerr (with barely five minutes on the clock) and then right at the end of the 90 minutes, that man Maloney had the last word when his perfectly judged free-kick sailed into the Motherwell net, confirming Celtic would return to Hampden to contest the final.

CIS Cup Final – Celtic 3 Dunfermline 0

Every Celtic player wore the number 7 on their shorts as a tribute to Jimmy Johnstone and it was surely fitting that it was the man with number 7 also on his back who broke the deadlock to send the Hoops on the way to victory. Dunfermline had been beaten 8-1 the previous month and boss Jim Leishman sent his side out determined to avoid a repeat performance. Celtic pressed hard from the first whistle but could not break through a resolute defence until the 43rd minute when Zurawski took advantage of a mix-up in the Dunfermline defence to side-foot home from close range and put the Bhoys in front.

Having established a lead, Celtic played some mesmerising football in the second half in an attempt to put the game beyond their opponents with Nakamura, Petrov and Maloney delighting the Celtic support with their trickery and skill. Less than fifteen minutes remained before the destination of the old trophy was put beyond doubt when Maloney, capping an excellent display, placed a free-kick from outside the penalty area over the defensive wall and into the net. There was still time for Dion Dublin to score his first goal for the club with a neat near-post finish in the final minute.

Skipper Neil Lennon, who along with his colleagues changed into a jersey with 'Johnstone 7' on the back, lifted the first trophy of the Strachan era and sparked great celebrations on the pitch and in the stands.

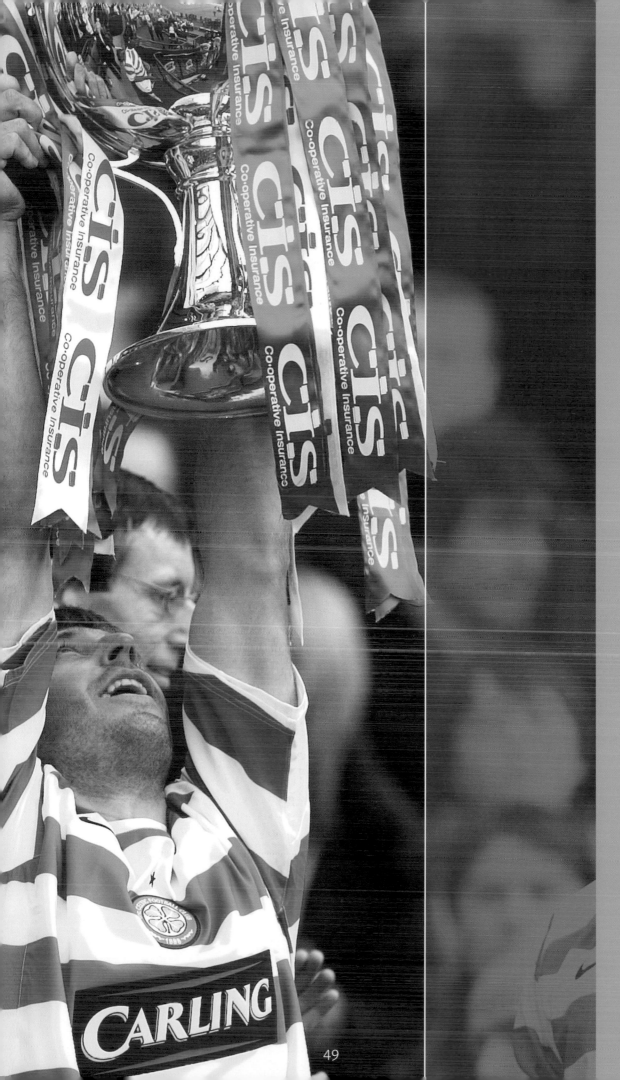

CIS CUP

Celtic One Member

Celtic One Member is the name of the new and improved Celtic World Huddle, the official global Celtic membership scheme. As well as the great gift pack and membership benefits you'd expect, being a Junior member puts you in with a chance of being selected to walk out of the Celtic Park tunnel on a matchday as an official mascot or ball boy/girl!

Celtic One Membership gives you great benefits such as a priority booking period before any public sale of gold dust tickets for the UEFA Champions League, as well as priority for home and away SPL games and domestic cup matches. You'll also be entered into exclusive prize draws throughout the season and Junior members can win places at the Celtic Junior Christmas party!

When you join, you'll be sent an exclusive gift pack relating to the type of membership you have. Adult members will receive a personal membership gift card; a metal gift tin; a metal pen; a metal clock and a metal keychain, and they'll also be entitled to a 5% discount in official Celtic shops on selected merchandise, 10% off Friday night bookings in the Number 7 Restaurant and a discount on holidays booked directly with Thomas Cook. Junior members, who must be aged under 16 on 3rd August 2006, will receive a personal membership card; plastic club folder; Celtic sticker set; bucket hat; birthday and Christmas cards and the same great discounts as adult members. Toddler members, who must be aged under 3 on 3rd August 2006, get a souvenir Hoopy drawstring bag; inflatable frisbee; Hoopy knife & fork set & Hoopy beanie hat, as well as the chance to have their pictures featured in the matchday programme or newsletter!

For the toddlers

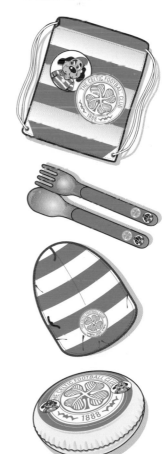

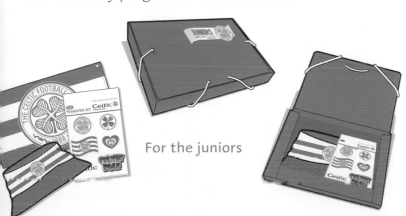

For the juniors

CELTIC ONE MEMBER

Celtic in the Community's top team of youth coaches have been letting bhoys and ghirls across Scotland and Ireland train and play the Celtic way since the summer of 2003, and the choice of courses on offer just keeps growing!

Budding Hoops aged from 3 to 16 can get involved in these fun courses, which are available during all school terms and holidays. There's also specialist coaching for goalkeepers, girls-only courses, and our residential coaching camps in the Easter and summer school holidays, complete with stadium visits and individual Academy player diaries, give a taste of the life of a professional player!

Celtic in the Community is the first level of the youth development programme at Celtic, which has already produced great players like Shaun Maloney and Aiden McGeady, with more on the way in the dominant Reserve and Under 19 sides. Celtic scouts attend coaching courses and have already invited promising young players into the Development Centres and the Youth Academy itself!

With the emphasis on fun and enjoyment, Celtic in the Community courses are an ideal way for young Hoops of all abilities to enjoy playing football, keep fit and healthy and make new friends.

Celtic in the Community runs courses throughout Scotland and Ireland and is always looking for new locations, so keep checking www.celticfc.net for news on the Community programme!

WORLD HUDDLE

Derek Riordan

The Edinburgh born striker has been a revelation at Hibernian and speculation over his future reached fever pitch when it became clear he planned to move on. Celtic fans were understandably delighted when it was announced in May that he would be signing for Celtic, particularly as Rangers had a bid for him turned down months before.

It was during the 2003/04 league campaign that he first came into the public eye with a string of impressive displays for the Easter Road outfit. His exceptional talent was underlined the following season when he netted 23 goals making him the top scoring Scottish player in the SPL for that year. He was also named the PFA Scottish Young Player of the Year for 2005.

A return of 63 goals in 117 top-flight appearances persuaded Gordon Strachan to move to make the youngster – now a Scotland international - the latest addition to the squad at Celtic Park.

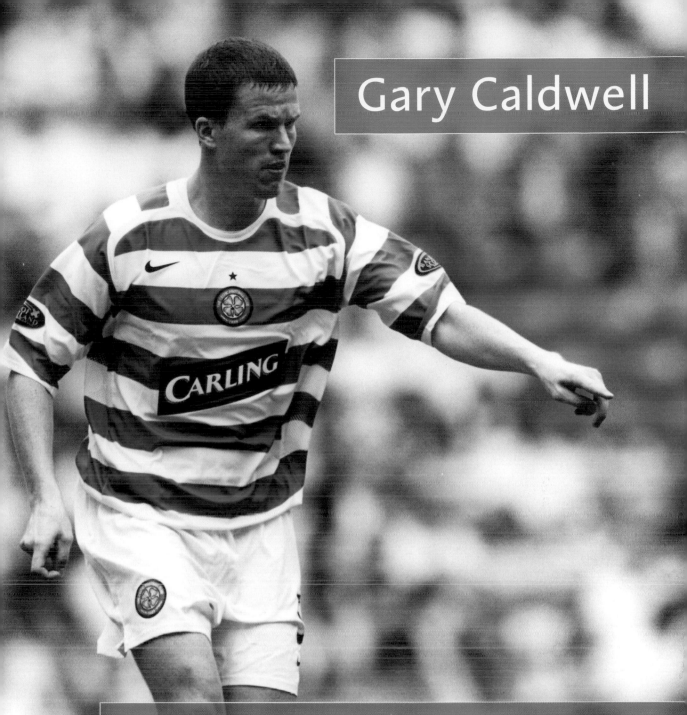

Gary Caldwell

A vital part of the Hibs side that impressed last season, the 24-year-old from Stirling played 34 league matches for the Edinburgh outfit as they pushed for a UEFA Cup berth. However in January it was confirmed that from June 2006 he would be plying his trade at Celtic Park having signed a pre-contract agreement.

The former Newcastle United player had been watched for some time by the Hoops management and they were understandably delighted to get their man. Celts' new No.5 was just as excited - pointing out he had "wanted to play here all my life".

Having been brought up playing football "the Celtic way" he is an advocate of passing the ball and good attacking football, indeed, the manager's commitment to a flowing, attractive style was a major factor in the Scotland international's decision to relocate along the M8 from Edinburgh. Gary has said his goal is "to win trophies and become part of Celtic's history" and if he shows the same commitment to this goal as he shows on the pitch he will surely achieve it.

Evander Sno

The Hoops had been watching the highly-rated Dutch teenager for over a year before finally capturing his signature. The utility man had been used in numerous positions at his previous club, NAC Breda, but upon signing him, Gordon Strachan was quick to mention that he had earmarked a central midfield role for the former Ajax and Feyenoord youngster.

The player himself, who was named after former Boxing champion, Evander Holyfield, is clearly relishing life in Glasgow saying: "I think it will be great for me to play here".

Jiri Jarosik

Having moved to Chelsea from CSKA Moscow in 2005 the Czech international struggled to break into the Stamford Bridge side's first 11 and was subsequently loaned out to Birmingham City. In the midlands he began to show the form which had attracted the Premiership giants to the tall midfielder (he stands at 6ft 4in). He featured 32 times for Steve Bruce's men and finished the season as the club's joint top-scorer.

This was enough, to persuade the Hoops' boss to swoop and he put pen to paper on a deal in June 2006. The manager was quick to point out his "tremendous ability and experience of playing at the highest level", experience which is bound to prove invaluable as Celtic mount their assault on Europe in 2006/07.

European Cup

Champions:	1966-67
Vice Champions:	1969-70
Semi Finalists:	1971-72, 1973-74
Quarter Finals:	1968-69, 1970-71, 1979-80

UEFA Cup

Finalists:	2002-2003
Quarter Finals:	2003-2004

Scottish League

Champions: 40 times

1892-93, 1893-94, 1895-96, 1897-98, 1904-05, 1905-06, 1906-07, 1907-08, 1908-09, 1909-10, 1913-14, 1914-15, 1915-16, 1916-17, 1918-19, 1921-22, 1925-26, 1935-36, 1937-38, 1953-54, 1965-66, 1966-67, 1967-68, 1968-69, 1969-70, 1970-71, 1971-72, 1972-73, 1973-74, 1976-77, 1978-79, 1980-81, 1981-82, 1985-86, 1987-88, 1997-98, 2000-01, 2001-02, 2003-04, 2005-06

Scottish Cup

Winners: 33 times

1892, 1899, 1900, 1904, 1907, 1908, 1911, 1912, 1914, 1923, 1925, 1927, 1931, 1933, 1937, 1951, 1954, 1965, 1967, 1969, 1971, 1972, 1974, 1975, 1977, 1980, 1985, 1988, 1989, 1995, 2001, 2004, 2005

League Cup

Winners: 13 times

1956-57, 1957-58, 1965-66, 1966-67, 1967-68, 1968-69, 1969-70, 1974-75, 1982-83, 1997-98, 1999-00, 2000-01, 2005-06

SPL Season 2005/06 Quiz (page 17)

1: 91
2: Shaun Maloney
3: David Fernandez
4: Dunfermline
5: Maciej Zurawski
6: Motherwell
7: Kilmarnock
8: Stephen Pearson
9: 18
10: Stephen McManus
11: Mark Wilson
12: Kilmarnock

Wordsearch (page 44)

Spot the Difference (page 21)

Champion's League Quiz (page 27)

1: 3
2: St Patrick's Athletic, 0-0
3: Mark Viduka
4: Joos Valgaeren, Henrik Larsson & Chris Sutton (2)
5: Anderlecht
6: John Hartson
7: Samuel Eto'o
8: Alan Thompson, John Hartson, Stephen McManus, Craig Beattie
9: Shota Arveladze
10: Liam Miller

Guess Who? (page 20)

1: John Hartson
2: Artur Boruc
3: Neil Lennon
4: Stilian Petrov
5: Paul Telfer
6: Stephen McManus

Anagram (page 45)

1: Billy McNeill
2: Shaun Maloney
3: Gordon Strachan
4: Shunsuke Nakamura
5: Paul Telfer
6: David Marshall
7: Aiden McGeady
8: Gary Caldwell
9: Jiri Jarosik
10: Ross Wallace